Healing The Wounded Child Within

To Unleash Your Inner "G"

By

LaDonna N. Smith

© Copyright 2022 by LaDonna N. Smith

All rights reserved.

This document is geared towards providing exact and reliable information with regards to the topic and issue covered. The publication is sold with the idea that the publisher is not required to render accounting, officially permitted, or otherwise, qualified services. If advice is necessary, legal or professional, a practiced individual in the profession should be ordered.

From a Declaration of Principles which was accepted and approved equally by a Committee of the American Bar Association and a Committee of Publishers and Associations.

In no way is it legal to reproduce, duplicate, or transmit any part of this document in either electronic means or in printed format. Recording of this publication is strictly prohibited and any storage of this document is not allowed unless with written permission from the publisher. All rights reserved.

The information provided herein is stated to be truthful and consistent, in that any liability, in terms of inattention or otherwise, by any usage or abuse of any policies, processes, or directions contained within is the solitary and utter responsibility of the recipient reader. Under no circumstances will any legal responsibility or blame be held against the publisher for any reparation, damages, or monetary loss due to the information herein, either directly or indirectly.

Respective authors own all copyrights not held by the publisher.

The information herein is offered for informational purposes solely, and is universal as so. The presentation of the information is without contract or any type of guarantee assurance. The trademarks that are used are without any consent, and the publication of the trademark is without permission or backing by the trademark owner. All trademark and brands within this book are for clarifying purposes only and are the owned by the owners themselves, not affiliated with this document.

For general information contact:

LaDonna N. Smith

Books to Hook Publishing, LLC

995 NW 119th Street STE 681186

North Miami, Florida 33168

800-576-3911

ISBN: 978-1-956525-45-8 *(Print)*

ISBN: 978-1-956525-46-5 *(eBook)*

DISCLAIMER

The author is not a health care professional or medical professional and the contents of this book are for informational purposes only. Whilst the information and opinions found in this book are written based on information available at the time of writing, and are believed to be accurate according to the best discernment of the author, the content is not intended to be a substitute for professional medical advice, diagnosis, or treatment. Any health concern must be assessed by a doctor. If you think you require assessment, call your doctor or local emergency department immediately. Reliance on any information provided by the author or the contents of this book is solely at your own risk.

Healing the Wounded Child Within to Unleash Your Inner "G"

Are you ready to UNLEASH YOUR INNER "G"? You're invited to step into your power, by working on letting go of old traumas so that you can reconnect with your higher self. You will learn how to Unleash your Inner "G" by doing the work to heal and awaken so you can transform your life. If you're ready to fight your inner demons and show them just how gangsta you are, this workbook is for you…

Table of Contents

Introduction 1

What is Inner Child Healing 2

How Does Inner Child Healing Work 4

Signs You Have a Wounded Inner Child 6

Why Inner Child Healing Is Important 8

Finding The Root Cause Of Your Childhood Trauma 10

Understanding your Childhood Triggers and How to Heal Them 15

Uncovering Your Inner Child 19

Uncovering Your Adult Self 21

Connecting your Inner Child with your Adult Self 23

How do I Reparent Myself 26

Taking Care of Yourself - Healing Starts From Within, Radical Forgiveness of Yourself and Others 28

Conclusion 30

Activity Pages 31

Acknowledgments 154

References 155

Introduction

We all have all have an inner child inside of us. There have been numerous occasions when we have all let our inner child out. For example, we may occasionally observe people and wonder why they act like enraged children, why they cannot forget the past, have an adult conversation, or act maturely when triggered. This is often the inner child manifesting its self in our adult lives. When we "innerstand" that many of our behaviors as an adult actually stem from our childhood experiences, we are able to use inner child healing to address our unmet needs and start the healing process.

When our inner child's pain continues to be ignored, our wounds may manifest as rage, envy, a lack of self-confidence, ect. So, whenever we feel such feelings, we must remember that they are not ours. We often have these feelings because our inner child is hurting and suffering. Please understand that making a conscious decision to do inner child healing work to end toxic patterns that hinder your life or plague your bloodline, is no easy task. While your journey wont be easy, remember it's necessary to get through the test to make it to your testimony!!!

Happy Healing!!

What is Inner Child Healing

Our lives are made up of experiences. Right from when we are born, we start to experience the world, as a beautiful sanctuary. However, many of us also experience the world in ways that are not helpful to our development as human beings.

Our childhood is the time of our lives when we are most impressionable by our parents, older siblings, and the people around us. We take their word as gospel and their actions as personal.

If there are inconsistencies in behavior and words, we may turn out to not trust others, and grow up having trust issues in our relationships. Depending on the situation, it could also be anger, bottled up inside you, shame, or other feelings of inadequacy.

Our parents play a central role in all of this and their actions perhaps affect us the most in subtle and unconscious ways. We may end up manifesting and reacting in our adulthood based on experiences from our childhood. The inadequacies of our parents, the hurt they caused us, the shame we felt at school, or even the "I'm not enough" feeling that teachers made you feel at school, can become triggers in your adult life.

But it isn't very fair for us to live our adult lives from a child's perspective, allowing childhood experiences to determine how we react and relate with others and our own selves. We all know that changing the past is not something that we can do, but we can adjust our adult selves to live without defaulting to our childhood selves.

Through healing and re-parenting, we can change, treat ourselves better and live with others in harmony as it should be because the past is what it is; we are not able to change it. Still, we can surely use it as a tool to learn about ourselves and to make ourselves much better human beings.

As you re-parent your inner child, you can speak peace to your mind and emotions. The inner child, brain, and body were hurt, but these things didn't hurt your soul. When inner child healing work is done, your perfected soul will heal your inner child by providing it with comfort, security, attention, and the love it yearns for.

How Does Inner Child Healing Work

It's startling to learn that our happiness today is heavily influenced by experiences from our youth. You will be closer to a happy existence if you see your childhood experiences as a starting point for the future and become conscious of the past's effects on your current life. How you were raised and the relationships you had during those formative years impact how well-adjusted you are and how you make decisions as an adult.

Your inner child is a friendly, joyous, passionate, free, and playful side of you. It depicts the young kid you once were, who needs affection and comfort, and it mixes your most primal emotions, your sensitivity, and creativity, which you were born with but may have hidden as you grew up.

The inner child is the human's childish feature, and it is influenced by all you learned and experienced as a child. Being aware of your inner child, a semiindependent entity that reports to your conscious mind, can help you better your life. Your inner child is your essence, the natural innocent, unsophisticated, and playful component of your awareness.

Inner Child Healing Work is a healing-centered method to working with individuals who have been subjected to many aspects of trauma including neglect, or mental, physical, or emotional abuse, just to name a few.

Inner Child Healing Work Combines a variety of psychological frameworks, including Jungian Shadow work, Psychoanalytic Psychotherapy, Internal Family Systems Therapy, and Somatic Experiencing Therapy.

Combining these psychological frameworks will allow individuals to explore their emotions, behaviors, unconscious patterns, and the family dynamics or early experiences rooted in the trauma they're living out in their adult life.

Signs You Have a Wounded Inner Child

We all have a child inside of us. If you had a happy childhood, your inner-child is most likely carefree and playful. However, if you were neglected or abused as a child, your inner child is highly likely to be damaged.

Most of us grow up completely oblivious that we have a wounded inner child. The main issue for much of our suffering is the fact that we aren't aware of the severity our own wounds. As a result, we are unlikely to notice that our wounded inner child is to blame for some of the unpleasant aspects of our lives.

It's critical to know where we originate regarding our negative behaviors and patterns. Recognizing our inner-child will assist us in better understanding ourselves as a whole, our behaviors, and the healing needed, thereby allowing us to grow into better versions of ourselves.

Tell, tale, signs ...

1. Do you struggle with trust? You can't trust anyone, including yourself. This is a sign that your inner child has been hurt. This could explain why you're frightened of getting hurt again if you allow someone to get too close to you. Lack of trust will have a detrimental impact on your relationships.
2. You have a severe fear of abandonment: This can manifest itself in various waysin your life. Due to your fear of abandonment, you may become co-dependent, nervous, develop anxiety, and even become angry toward your partner. This behavior comes with some serious consequences.
3. You are vulnerable to addiction: Addiction can take many forms, including food,drugs, alcohol, and even sex. Addiction is a form of self-medication that

occurs due to unresolved trauma or pain.

4. The trouble with addiction is that the pain persists, yet you are exacerbating it by refusing to accept yourself.

5. You have difficulty when it comes to setting boundaries: It is imperative to set boundaries for adulthood unless you want to be at the mercy of others. Children who have been through trauma are conditioned to believe that their feelings are unimportant. They grow up not knowing how to set healthy boundaries or limits that ensure toxic individuals are kept at bay.

To avoid friction with others, you people-please: People-pleasers compromise their own feelings and needs for those around them to avoid conflict. This could be the outcome of a childhood in which your needs and feelings were silenced and undervalued. It's as if you're repeating what you were subjected to as a child. These are just a few signs that you may be dealing with a wounded inner child. What can you do if these things seem familiar? The first step, they say, is admitting that your inner child exists and facing their pain.

Why Inner Child Healing Is Important

A catastrophic event impacts a person's life. The effects are usually more severe if the trauma is persistent; nonetheless, even a single encounter might cause irreversible damage. Whether your childhood trauma was the result of witnessing a traumatic accident or, as is more common, being the victim of physical, sexual, or serious emotional abuse, you have almost certainly already suffered the consequences.

One of the most crucial things to remember is that the effects do not have to be long-term. What happened to you as a child does not have to negatively impact the rest of your life! You also don't have to spend the rest of your life relying on support groups or drugs, therapy or counseling, or any of the other ways that are becoming increasingly fashionable these days. While such tactics can be beneficial in the short term, they can also lead to dependency. The bottom line is that they can keep you stuck in the problem rather than affording you a real solution.

Childhood trauma can result in a slew of issues. Examples are eating disorders, substance abuse, failure to build and sustain healthy relationships, and other issues. A trauma survivor may feel helpless and hopeless due to these issues.

Living in the solution entails addressing the root cause of these issues. You've made headway toward a solution when you can face the trauma and recognize it for what it was. You're taking the best steps toward letting go when you work through all of those feelings of pain, rage, and uncertainty.

If you haven't followed these measures yet, you still suffer from the trauma's effects. When old sentiments are not addressed in the context of the trauma, they frequently manifest in other, highly inappropriate ways. You don't have to keep repeating this pattern, nor do you have to make rehabilitation your only goal for the rest of your life.

If you were traumatized during your childhood, you might be at a crossroads right now. You may be ready to admit how harmful those experiences were to you in the long run and the impact they had on almost every aspect of your life.

If you're ready to make some positive changes and start living in the solution rather than the problem, the good news is that you're on your way to a brighter and more fulfilling future.

Are you ready to leave the past behind you and be free of its repercussions? Be wary of anything that appears to add to your dependency - whether it's keeping the old problem or creating new ones; it's not the solution.

Some answers are not only more positive but also better in the long run - the best of which is that your life can finally be in your own hands, to live and experience as you desire! All of this may be yours once you start living in the solution!

Finding The Root Cause Of Your Childhood Trauma

Isolated incidences such as accidents, injuries, or a violent attack can create emotional and psychological stress, especially during childhood. Continuous stressors such as living in a dangerous area, suffering a life-threatening illness, bullying, domestic violence, or early childhood trauma such as maltreatment could all contribute to the trauma.

A romantic breakup, surgery, a frustrating event, and a humiliating situation are all examples of triggering situations that don't appear to be very serious to most people. However, these instances, might be more difficult for a trauma survivor. So, understanding how childhood trauma affects adulthood can help you empathize with yourself and other survivors.

The death of a parent, caregiver, or close relative

Children tend to cling to their parents, guardians, grandparents, or anybody else in the family with whom they feel safe. Children's instincts are to cling to their elders for safety, protection, and support. For any child, the death of a loved one is devastating. It's difficult for a child to cope with sadness when they realize they won't see their loved one again. It is important to speak with your children about a death in the family. It is critical to communicate. In many instances, childhood trauma can be avoided with prompt attention.

Betrayed trust

Children become reliant on their caregivers or anyone else with whom they feel at ease, and they begin to place their greatest faith in them. Friends, family friends, school teachers, classmates, and other individuals may be there in addition to caretakers and family members.

Regardless of the person, if a child is betrayed or feels betrayed, he or she may develop mistrust even in little ways. It may not be traumatizing every time, but it will be if the level of betrayal is high or frequent. Children who have had their trust betrayed may also grow up thinking toxic behavior patterns in relationships are acceptable.

Living in Poverty

Poverty may not be a problem for everyone; otherwise, over half of the world's population would be traumatized. On the other hand, living in poverty can significantly impact a child's behavior and cognitive process. Depending on the individual, the impact might be both beneficial and bad. The child may be traumatized as a result of the negative effect. Childhood trauma can be caused by various factors, including regular powerlessness, a lack of money, food insecurity, housing instability, or having parents who work long hours, and so forth.

Abuse

Childhood is the most important time in one's life. Children are exposed to various tiny and large situations, some of which affect them greatly and others that do not. Unfortunately, some children are subjected to horrific maltreatment. Some of the possible abuses are physical, emotional, verbal, and sexual abuse. A child is most likely to be abused at home, at school, or in their neighborhood. In many cases, abusers tend to be individuals that are supposed to safeguard the children, such as their parents, teachers, guardians, or other caregivers.

The child may experience constant verbal abuse in comments or inappropriate language. "You're stupid," "You shouldn't be alive," and a slew of other phrases come to mind. Verbal abuse can be fatal. It affects a child's belief system, and they may begin to believe that they are unworthy of living.

Children may also suffer physical harm. Aside from common childhood injuries, a child can suffer long-term consequences from the physical abuse experienced during their childhood. Depending on the frequency and intensity, maltreatment and neglect can impede a child's physical development or lead to psychological issues such as depression, suicidal thoughts, low self-esteem, substance abuse, and more.

Sexual abuse can take the form of a forced act by a family member or another adult. The most common kind of sexual abuse is incest. Abuse in the family, or the degree of abuse, is a common source of depression, guilt, shame, self-blame, anxiety, eating disorders, and various other problems. Any human being's fundamental rights are violated when sexually abused as children. It can stifle social development and lead to a slew of psychosocial issues.

Pain

The child may have had any medical procedure or pain. The discomfort might be excruciating. Are you considering how pain can be a source of trauma? In that situation, you should keep in mind that while you can tolerate pain as an adult, children are fragile and vulnerable. They have a hard time tolerating intense pain. They may be traumatized and in excruciating agony. Any such occurrence may cause them to acquire a severe fear or phobia.

Immigration and childhood Trauma

With all of the wandering and constant worry of persecution and violence, children who live as immigrants develop a unique form of terror or trauma. These children lack stability in their lives, whether in their schooling or their childhood living environment. They do not live their lives in the same way that other children do, making it difficult for them to adjust to any form of normalcy.

While this type of trauma is not a reality for all immigrants, for those it's true for, the trauma can have a detrimental effect on the child in many ways.

Natural disaster/war

War and natural calamities are stressful not only for children but also for adults. Any type of war or natural disaster is always devastating to those caught in the middle of it. It ruins everything, and the majority of affected people are the ones who survive. When the survivor is a child, such incidents might be quite traumatic. Unless they receive enough care and love, they may develop post-traumatic stress disorder (PTSD) or depressive symptoms.

Parents who have divorced

Parents are a child's most visible and vital source of mental support. On the other hand, divorce may be painful for the children for the rest of their lives. It is simple for the couple to get divorced. Children, however, are the ones who suffer the most in such situations. It's difficult for them to pick just one parent. It's also considerably more difficult for them to accept divorce. They may develop a negative belief system about marriage as a whole. Witnessing their parents' divorce may have an impact on their future relationships.

Bullying

Many people believe school, college, cyberbullying and even bullying at home are to be expected. Often, the child does not receive the required listening ear from his or her parents. Bullying can cause a child or teenager to have a traumatic life. Such events permanently traumatize children and diminish their confidence, self-esteem, and courage.

The child may experience fear and helplessness throughout his or her life. Many people commit suicide as a result of excessive bullying. They begin to doubt themselves, live a life of fear, and develop feelings of being a failure. The sheer fact that they cannot protect themselves, causes them to despise themselves, leading to self-doubt.

Serious Accident

Any catastrophic accident or medical emergency they may have experienced as children can leave them terrified for the rest of their lives. They aren't prepared to deal with such events in the future and have begun to isolate themselves from others. They begin to worry about being caught in a similar circumstance and mistrust their ability to escape. Furthermore, such events may leave a permanent scar or deformity on their bodies, reducing their confidence and self-esteem.

Having a sibling who is sick

They feel invisible because they have a sick sibling. It's only natural for the parents to devote more attention to the ill child. However, the other child may develop feelings of insecurity and jealousy due to this. They begin to feel ignored and shunned. As a result, individuals experience a form of trauma that may have a lasting emotional impact.

Being a witness to a serious crime

Murders, rapes, and gang violence have a profoundly emotional and traumatizing effect on children. The mere concept of such situations is so painful that one tries to avoid them at all costs. However, if a child observes such an occurrence, it is unlikely that they will ever forget it. They live in continual fear and trauma since, this is especially true if the horrible acts involved any of their loved ones.

Understanding your Childhood Triggers and How to Heal Them

If we've been through trauma in our life, we may find ourselves being triggered by people, places, or even things. We may even notice certain things that others do or say that cause us to act out or reflect on our own experiences throughout our lives.

We may even grow up to have comparable thoughts and feelings to those we were traumatized by, or we may be triggered by any similarities of their behavior displayed in others that we may come in contact with. For instance, when we grow up with a parent who loses control when angry, we may frequently lose control in situations or we may perceive an angry person as more of a risk than than they really are. Others' actions may also cause us to reflect on the person who has wounded us or the time when we have been hurt. All of these are "trauma triggers."

Some of our feelings may be tied to our prior experiences, which we are not always conscious of. We may feel terrified and bewildered without understanding why if we are unaware of the relationship between what just happened and what happened to us previously.

Those of us who belong to racial or ethnic groups that have endured historical trauma, such as slavery or genocide, are frequently subjected to racism, prejudice, and discrimination, leading to more trauma. These can include overt or covert systems or behaviors that discriminate against or hurt those who identify with these groups. Prejudicial words made by people who are either purposefully nasty or well-intentioned but oblivious of the harm they create are other examples.

Each new traumatic incident in our lives can serve as a reminder of previous ones. Each one may also serve as a reminder of the historical tragedy our ancestors endured, which our families have passed down to us. Re-traumatizing situations can reawaken feelings of anger, powerlessness, and a loss of control over who we actually are.

1. Recognize the emotions associated with trauma triggers

There are numerous approaches to dealing with our reactions to trauma triggers. We might begin by learning to recognize the feelings that can arise from trauma triggers. These feelings could include sudden fear or worry, shutting down and becoming silent, or running away from the situation. When triggered, we may notice that we have experienced similar feelings. Nonetheless, we may not realize the connection between those feelings and what happened to us in the past at the time.

2. Anticipate triggers by determining when they are most likely to occur

We can recognize and anticipate potential triggers in events and interactions. We may prepare for them and feel more in control if we do so. This can assure us that we won't be caught off guard. We can gain insight into what sets us off and how we react to these things.

As we progress, we may notice that these memories, ideas, and feelings no longer appear to creep up on us and influence our actions. We can decide what we want to do with those thoughts and feelings when we notice them manifesting.

This sensation of mastery and reclaiming control over what we think, feel, and do is vital for the healing process.

3. Make a self-care plan for when triggers occur

When we face a trauma trigger, one way to be prepared is to take a break and ask for support. Taking a break will allow us to gather our thoughts, regulate our emotions, and we can prepare what we will say ahead of time.

Finding a quiet, private area where we can take a few deep breaths and bring our thoughts back to the present moment may be enough to help us relax. We may also wish to coordinate with others who can lend support ahead of time to ensure that someone can assist us in times of distress.

If we require more than quiet time, we can employ other coping mechanisms that we are already familiar with. Getting in touch with a friend or loved one, going for a short walk outside, and looking for the positive aspects of the circumstance are all examples.

4. Seek out additional supports

Flashbacks, panic attacks, re-experiences of the trauma, and other consequences of what occurred to us may make it impossible for us to be with our family or live our lives as we would. If this occurs, we can seek the assistance of a mental health expert. However, we must remember that healing will be tough at times. Yet, setbacks do not indicate that we cannot heal or that we have failed. Rest assured that setbacks are a necessary part of the healing process.

5. Self-compassion is important

Learning to be patient and compassionate with yourself is one of the most critical aspects of childhood trauma healing. It was not your fault what occurred to you as a child. Even if the trauma you experienced as a child was caused by something you did, you were only a child. You had no idea what you were doing. Even if you did, you can't be held liable for something that happened so long ago. You must first learn to love and forgive yourself by loving and forgiving yourself. It would help if you learned to accept what has occurred without blaming yourself.

6. Recognize your triggers

Finally, knowing your emotional triggers is necessary for learning how to heal from childhood trauma. Learn what triggers self-destructive or damaging thought patterns, behaviors, and emotions. You can learn to avoid your triggers once you've discovered them. You can also learn how to prepare for them and deal with them if they're unavoidable.

7. Recognize the importance of your trauma in your life

Next, while facing the childhood trauma that has had such a deep impact on your life can be tough and unpleasant, you must accept it for what it is. It would help if you understood its significance in your daily life. This covers things like habits, feelings, mental patterns, and fears, among other things. You can learn to get past these patterns once you correlate them with your past experiences— understanding why is always beneficial.

Uncovering Your Inner Child

We lose touch with our inner child as we grow older. We are so eager to grow up as children that we often overlook the reality that there is still a child within us. Every one of us has an inner child begging for our attention. Your feelings are a common way your inner child will express its wants and needs. For instance, we may readily forgive a child who is terrified of social situations; nevertheless, the true tragedy occurs when this child has grown up and is still afraid and terrified. Here is where the inner child attempts to communicate with you that it requires attention and healing work. Even though you are in an adult body, you are still a child inside. Society, school, family, friends, government, and the media have all conditioned us to grow up and cease acting like children. However, while many of us have grown in age, we have not actually grown up. How many times have you heard someone tell you to "act your age?" Yes, we must be responsible adults, but there is a part of you that is still a child, and it is lashing out at you, pleading for attention and healing. Past events and current conditions can sometimes make the inner child fearful. So, as the adult, you must learn to console your inner child.

Have you ever noticed how nice you feel after having a funny experience? Laughter is a way for us to connect with our inner child. You've probably heard the saying that a cheerful heart is good medicine, and it's true. Being a grownup in today's stressful world is difficult. This is why it's so important to form a bond with your inner child.

This may appear unusual at first, but it works. This is a personal process that does not require the assistance of another individual. It's a battle between you and your inner child. Allow your inner child to feel secure in your company. The more you connect to who you truly are on the inside, the more you will gradually begin to notice you have a happier and more content inner child. As a result, the adult you also becomes happier.

As you create a connection with your inner child, you will notice the emptiness dissipate and addictive behavior decrease. The key to a happy existence is to connect to all parts of you. And connecting to your inner child is a required part of the process.

Set aside the adult and let your inner child loose when you have the opportunity. It will take some time getting used to, but you will notice how much better you feel once you start letting loose and doing these things that stir up positive emotions in both you and your inner child.

Have some fun with your inner child today!

Uncovering Your Adult Self

"Grow a pair." I realize it sounds harsh, but not many of us manage to mature into true grownups. The good news is that you have an adult within you waiting to makes its public debut. There are few real role models to look up to today. There are already many celebrities and many others with access to social media displaying their infantile antics and behaviors to the world.

Adult children, who, on the other hand, as adults, frequently feel small, fragile, voiceless, and powerless, must make friends with their adult self rather than their inner child. Our inner child is frequently so powerful that our adult self has little room to make good decisions and have healthy relationships in our lives. The inner child includes the part of us that feels worried, terrified, and powerless, while our adult self includes the calm, reasonable, and empowered part of us.

Being a witness to oneself is the first step. Take a step back and observe what you do, how you react, and who you become in different situations. Observe your thoughts. What thoughts lead you to speak, behave, and feel the way you do? Self-awareness is the act of observing oneself. This isn't the kind of selfcons ciousness where you're concerned about how you appear to others. This is what nonjudgmental self-awareness is all about. Pay attention to yourself and take notes.

As you observe yourself in various situations, are you a center of influence or a center of attention? Every thought, emotion, word, and behavior expressed by a center of influence has an effect. "What effect did my words, tone, or actions have on that person?" you ask yourself if you disagree with someone. You perceive others through the lens of their needs, not yours, as a center of influence. This is how a grownup views the world.

When you're the center of attention, you perceive other people and the world through the lens of what they've done to you or what they should be doing for you. You are the center of the universe. You perceive others through the lens of your wants, not theirs, when you're the center of attention. This is a child's perspective of the world, where your own ideas, feelings, words, and behaviors are at the center of your influence. Yet, you are aware of your influence.

There is no one to blame and nothing to be unhappy about. There are no justifications. You aren't a helpless victim. You are solely responsible for your actions. You set goals for yourself and either achieve them or fail. Failure is a chance to learn something new. You learn and move on after recognizing a mistake or acknowledging a failure. You don't hold yourself hostage to guilt, and you don't expect others to either. If you're living your life where you are the center of influence, it's up to you to do the healing work to change to ensure that you're not traumatizing others with your behaviors.

As an adult, you play multiple roles and live your life consciously. You play your role as a child, and life happens to you. Even as adults, we are still emotional beings who make errors. The distinction is between awareness and ownership. You catch yourself and rectify yourself. Managing your ego takes a lot of practice. Your ego combines your inner child and adult self, but it is not who you are.

You are the spectator, and the witness. Who exactly is this observer I'm talking about? That is a mature question, and I hope you continue to ask yourself this question during your healing process..

Connecting your Inner Child with your Adult Self

Everyone has a child within them. On the other hand, people occasionally forget to embrace the fun and lighthearted side of life. Reconnecting with your inner child entails a shift of perspective. Allowing yourself time to play, explore, laugh, and observe the world with delight and astonishment is what it implies.

Play!

Adult obligations, such as paying bills or running errands, can often cause you to take life too seriously. Now and then, everyone needs to come out of their shell.

Dance, sing, draw, or just relax. Have a water balloon fight with your friends. Have a fantastic time laughing at a comedy movie. Everyday events become intriguing, amusing, and enjoyable when you approach life with a lighthearted mindset!

You can utilize playfulness to relieve tension even when dealing with difficult situations, such as at work or during social encounters. This freespirited, joyful perspective provides a more positive outlook on life, allowing you to cope with stress in healthy ways.

Openly and honestly express oneself

Children appear to be unafraid to express themselves via dance, laughter, and play! They know how to tell it like it is, and they may be brutally honest at times! As you get older, society norms have a more substantial influence on your actions. You may grow timid or afraid to express yourself. You may be reluctant to speak up out of fear of being rejected.

Your true self is screaming for attention! You miss out on valuable connections and experiences when you hold back on expressing your true feelings. Learn to talk openly and honestly to rekindle the spirit of your inner child. It is fine if not everyone agrees with what you have to say. When you express yourself, you give the world your unique perspective and, as a result, you will attract people who like you.

Spend time with the kids

Spending more time with children is a great approach to bring out your inner child. Making time to spend with your kids, whether telling jokes, running around or playing games, helps you tap into your inner playfulness and youthful imagination. You also have the opportunity to contribute your knowledge to assist young people in learning and growing. If you don't have children of your own, you could spend time with the children of friends or family members.

Take pleasure in learning

Adults are more concerned with problem-solving and completing tasks. Children have an eagerness to study and discover the world's many possibilities. You can reconnect with your inner child by letting go of the constant drive to correct and control. Instead, have an open mind and look for learning opportunities every day.

Use your imagination

Children enjoy learning through arts and crafts, dance, coloring, singing, and other activities. You may also bring out your inner child through creative activities, which come with a slew of health benefits. Self-expression aids in the recovery from trauma, managing emotions, and promoting overall well-being.

Do you require some motivation? There are several adult coloring books available to get your creative juices flowing. Start some do-it-yourself tasks to decorate your home or office.

Heal your inner child's wounds

Early in life, much of your personality and habits are formed. You may unconsciously continue to act out habits learned as a child as you get older. When you're stuck in life, you may need to repair your wounded inner child. Cognitive behavioral therapists frequently have patients reconnect with their inner child to heal themselves of maladaptive emotional and behavioral patterns acquired as children.

It is necessary to repair old wounds to break negative cycles.

Close your eyes for a moment. Consider yourself as a small child again. What would you say to reassure that child? You can even write a letter to your inner child to guide him or her. This practice will aid in healing old wounds and the development of self-compassion. When you perceive yourself as a child, it'll be simpler to forgive yourself for the mistakes you've made.

To be a true adult, you must nourish and listen to your inner child. It means to pay attention to prior hurts, respond to their needs, and heal. You become more aware of the motivations underlying your behaviors, emotions, and relationships through the inner-awareness process, when you reconnect with your inner child.

How do I Reparent Myself

Children are not only reliant on their parents and caregivers for fundamental necessities. The adults in your life also teach you how to recognize, express, and control your emotions and set limits, relax, and be kind. You'll likely struggle with your emotions and behaviors as an adult if you weren't exposed to unconditional love and healthy relationship as a child.

In this light, re-parenting oneself entails providing yourself with the emotional support you lacked as a child. You could believe that social and emotional abilities come naturally. You may be missing out on something that others appear to have or understand. But keep in mind that they are merely exhibiting learned habits. It's not too late to start learning and treating yourself with the respect and care you deserve. Learning to satisfy your own needs and support yourself with love and compassion is exactly what re-parenting yourself is all about.

There are a variety of techniques to re-parent yourself and reconnect with your inner child. Here are a few helpful techniques:

1. Recognize that you have an inner child

Only until you've acknowledged that your inner child exists and that it may be wounded can you begin to heal. Try to recollect any traumatic memories that have lingered in your mind to this day. Discovering these wounds will help you better understand how they have affected your adult self.

2. Pay attention to your inner child and allow it to speak to you

Sadness, rage, humiliation, guilt, fear, and anxiety are some of the challenging feelings that can arise when you connect with your inner child. Try to connect these to specific events from your childhood to see where they came from.

3. Write your inner child a letter

It may seem foolish, but writing to your inner child as an adult can be very beneficial in relieving your pain. For example, you may have wondered why your sister mistreated you as a child and now believe you know the reason. It's possible that hearing it will help your inner child heal.

4. Try writing in a journal and meditating

These hobbies can enhance your physical and emotional health in various ways. They can help you become more self-aware, open your mind, and work through difficult situations.

5. Reconnect with your child like side

Playfulness and relaxation are important aspects of emotional well-being. Daily, you may be concerned about your career, social life, and other adult responsibilities. Many positive feelings can be rekindled by bringing back the lightheartedness and delights of childhood.

6. Recognize that re-parenting is an ongoing process

Your healing journey doesn't have to conclude. It's a never-ending process. If you keep listening to your inner child, giving it compassion and love, and working on healing your wounds, you will learn something new everyday.

7. Consult a relationship counselor

It's difficult to re-parent yourself. This is why it is a good idea to speak with a compassionate and knowledgeable specialist who can provide you with guidance and insight as you embark on your healing journey.

Taking Care of Yourself - Healing Starts From Within, Radical Forgiveness of Yourself and Others

It's frequently easier said than done to make peace and move forward. Empathy, compassion, kindness, and understanding are all necessary qualities for self-forgiveness. It also necessitates your acceptance of the fact that forgiving is a choice. The actions you need to take to forgive yourself will look and feel the same whether you're attempting to work through a small traumatic event or one that has far-reaching consequences.

1. Concentrate on your feelings

Focusing on your emotions is one of the first steps in learning to forgive yourself. You must acknowledge and process your feelings before you can move on. Allow yourself to accept, embrace, and welcome the feelings that have been awakened in you.

2. Acknowledge the mistake out loud

If you've made a mistake and are having trouble letting it go, say out loud what you've learned from it. You may be able to liberate yourself from some of the burdens if you give voice to the thoughts in your head and the emotions in your heart. You can also imprint what you learned from your actions and consequences in your mind.

3. Give yourself permission to put this process on hold

If you make a mistake and have trouble letting go, envision your thoughts and feelings that you need to let go of being put into a box.

Then convince yourself you're putting this aside for the time being and will return to it if and when it's beneficial to you.

4. Have a dialogue with your inner critic

Journaling can aid in the understanding of your inner critic as well as the development of self-compassion. You can start by writing a "dialogue" between yourself and your inner critic. This might assist you in identifying toxic mental patterns that prevent you from forgiving yourself.

You can also use your journaling time to compile a list of traits you admire in yourself, such as your strengths and abilities. Save your journal entries. When you're feeling bad about a mistake you've made or yourself, reading the previous journal entry can make you feel more confident.

5. Make a list of what you want

If you made a mistake that caused harm to another person, you must decide what the best course of action is. Do you wish to speak with this person and express your regret? Is it necessary to make amends and reconcile with them? If you're undecided about what to do, you should think about making amends. This goes beyond apologizing to someone you've wronged. Instead, strive to correct the error you've made. It's easier to forgive ourselves for hurting someone else if we first make amends.

6. Show compassion and kindness

It's time to show yourself some warmth and compassion if your initial reaction to a terrible scenario is to criticize yourself. Being nice and sympathetic to yourself is the only way to start the process of forgiveness. This takes time, patience, and a constant reminder that you are forgiven.

Conclusion

Each of us has an inner child. Many of us are inadvertently merged with our inner child and are unaware of it. Our adult perspective can "merge" with the inner story of the wounded inner child, including intense negative emotions, distorting our image of ourselves and the world around us, especially during times of stress. If left unchecked, we can repeat the traumas we've encountered in the past.

Countless people worldwide grow up believing that something is wrong with them due to things that occurred in their past. It's critical to recognize that childhood traumas (and the consequences of those traumas) do not define you.

Activity Pages

The following activity pages contain a collection of exercises designed to support you on your healing journey. For an optimal experience, use these activity pages as you follow along with the 21-Day Virtual Re-Parenting Challenge (optional).

Sign up for the challenge at: www.innergholistichealing.com/thr-courses/

Intention Setting Worksheet

Life is made up of choices and your choices help determine what you experience in your life. Remember, no one owes you anything, but you owe yourself everything!

"Our intentions create our reality."
-Wayne Dyer-

Childhood Timeline……

1	2
3	4
5	6

What Is The Theme Song Of Your Life?

Theme: The Main Message, Basis, Story, or Central Idea of Something.

Why did you choose this as your Theme Song?

_____
_____
_____
_____

Reality Check

Sometimes we think our childhood trauma does not really impact our adult lives. However, this couldn't be further from the truth. Give yourself a reality check. Use the page below to write down a few examples of how your inner child shows up in your adult life.

_____

_____

_____

_____

_____

_____

_____

_____

_____

_____

Inner Child Drawing

use the space provided to draw a photo of your inner child. However, use your non-dominant hand to draw. It is believed that using your non-dominant hand provides more access to right brain functions like feelings, intuition, spirituality, and creativity. Let's see what you can come up with!

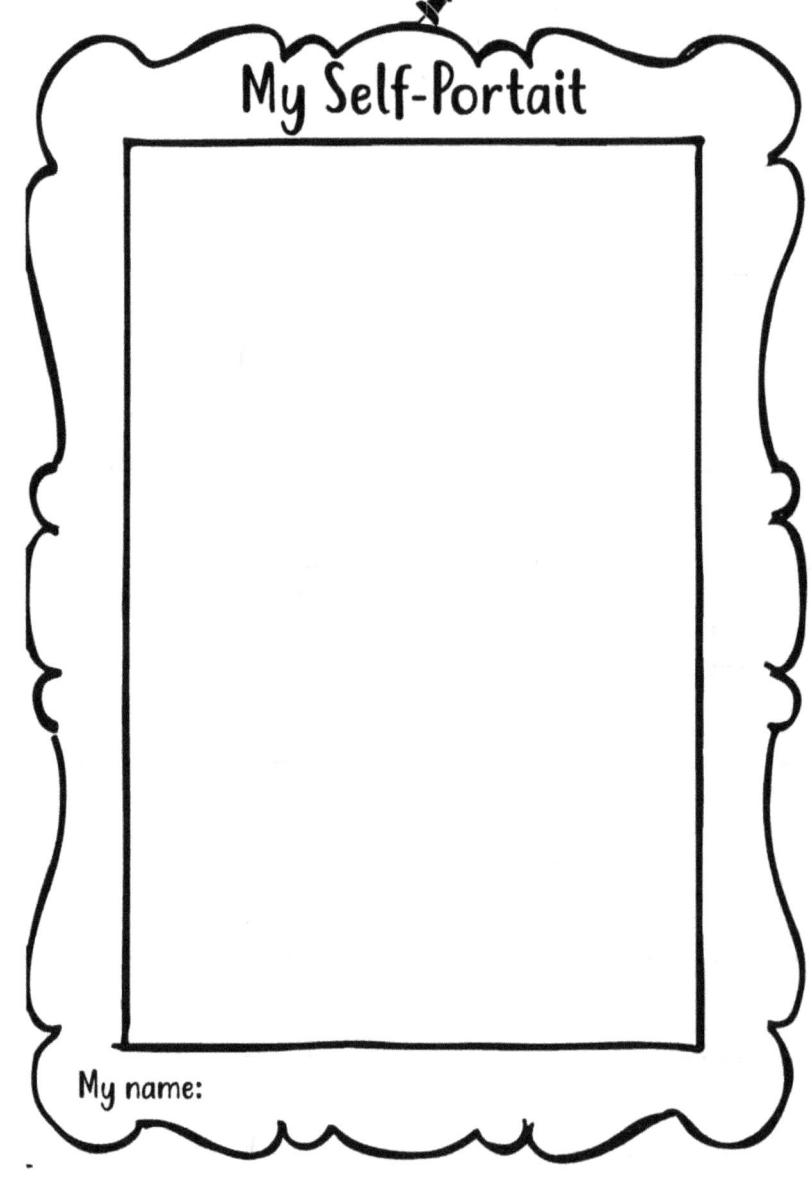

My Self-Portait

My name:

Let's Play Q&A...

Have your inner child ask your adult self questions.
Have your adult self ask your inner child questions.
Answer the questions on the next page...

Child Self	Adult Self

Let's Play Q&A...

Answer the questions...

_____

| Child Self | Adult Self |

My Family Tree

Let's Get To The Root Of Things: Use the family tree to fill in the names of your direct family members. Also, include a little about the type of relationship you had with each family member. For instance, was the relationship loving, toxic, hostile, non-existent, etc.? Use the next few pages to write in more detail about your family relationships.

Getting to the root of things...

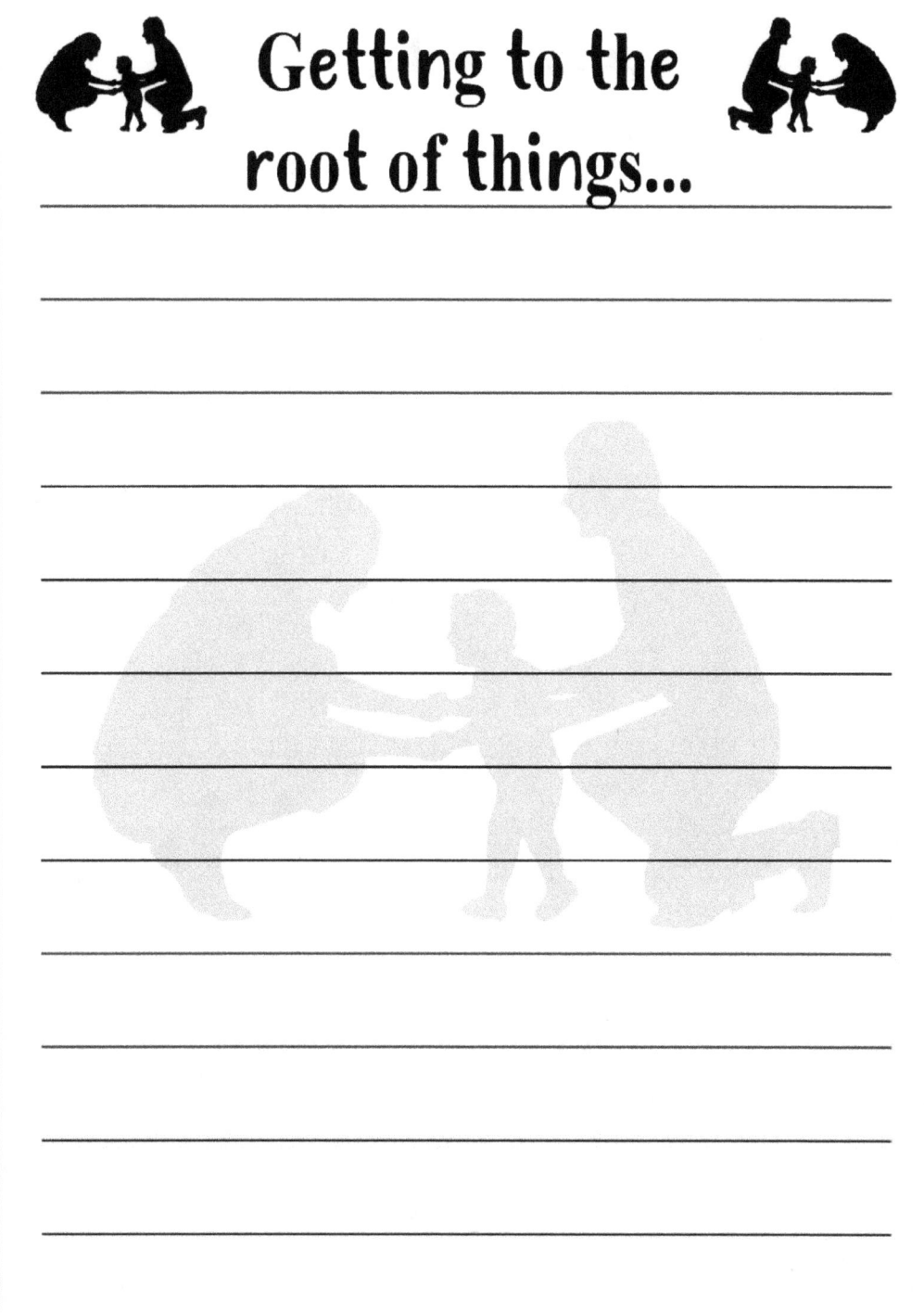

Getting to the root of things...

Getting to the root of things...

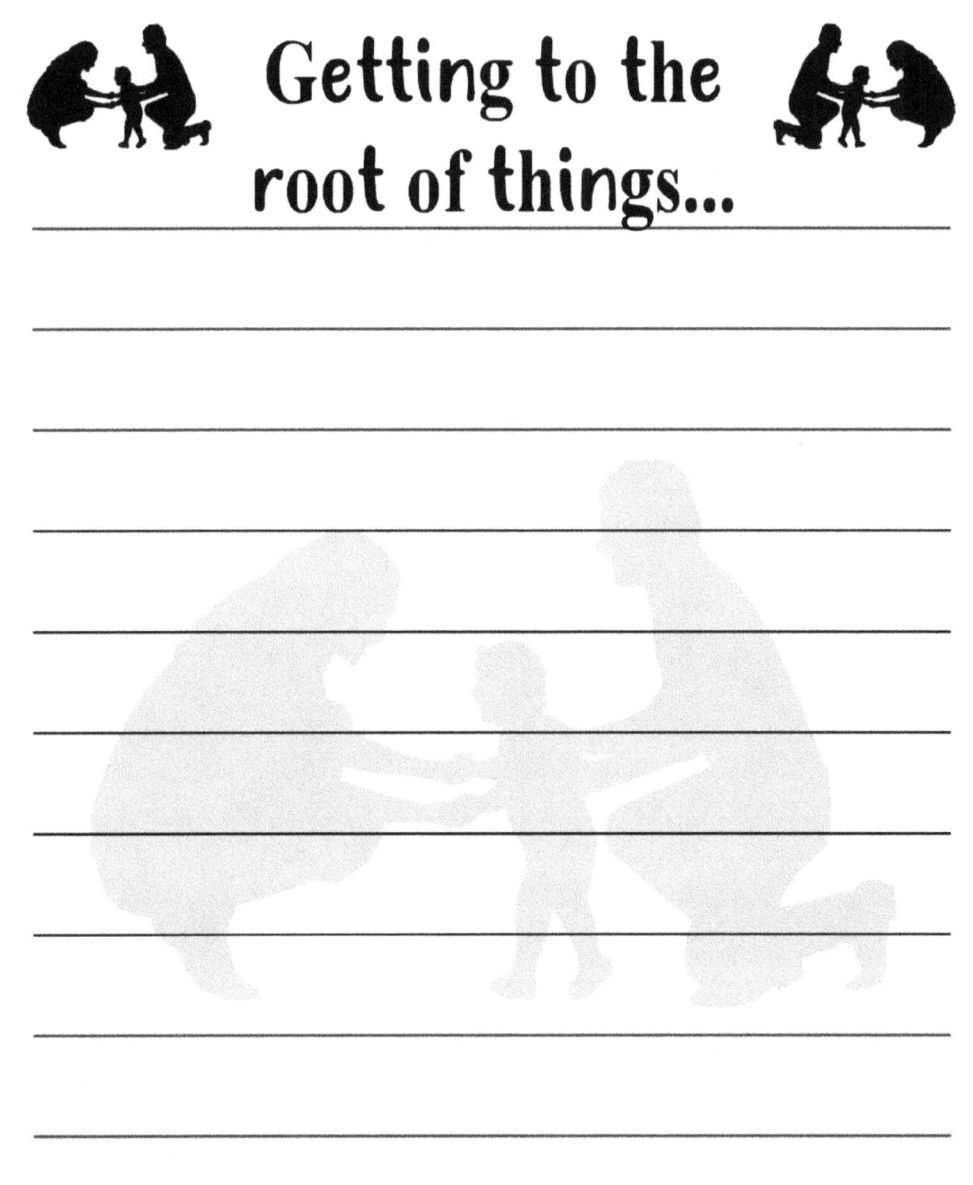

Getting to the root of things...

What relationships in your life require healing?

What are some emotional memories you need to heal most?

How was your relationship with your mother as a child?

What is a great memory you have about your relationship with your mother?

What is the most painful memory you have of your mother?

Is there anything you always wanted to ask your mother but were afraid to ask?

Are there any triggers that come up when thinking of the relationship with your mother?

What did you love and admire about your mother?

What kind of mother do you want to be to your inner child?

How was your relationship with your father as a child?

What is a great memory you have about your relationship with your father?

What is the most painful memory you have of your father?

Is there anything you always wanted to ask your father but were afraid to ask?

Are there any triggers that come up when thinking of the relationship with your father?

_____

_____

_____

_____

_____

_____

_____

_____

_____

_____

_____

_____

_____

_____

_____

_____

_____

What did you love and admire about your father?

What kind of father do you want to be to your inner child?

Write down 10 of your favorite childhood memories.

The house that Gratitude Built!

Although we're working on healing childhood trauma, not everything that happened in our childhood was bad. Are there some things you experienced or learned in your childhood that you're grateful for? Maybe there was a person who made a positive impact on your life. Use the house to list things you're grateful for.

What other message does your inner child want to give you about growing up in this home?

What Would I Take With Me?

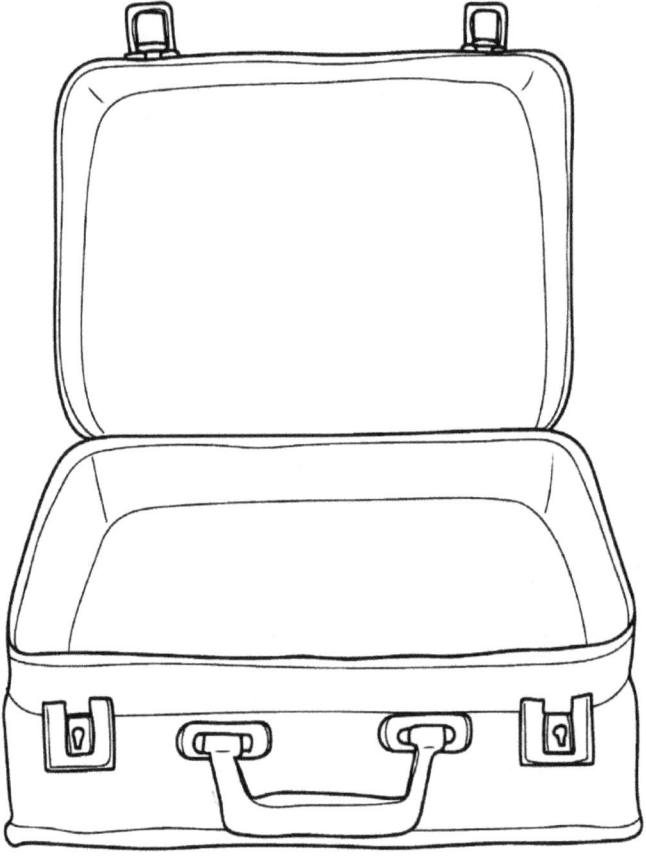

- **Why?**

_____
_____
_____
_____

There are some important lessons in life that we are only taught through difficult times, and they can become critical aspects of our growth. What positive attributes can you take away from your negative experience?

What Was Said Versus What I Needed To Hear?

At times the adults in our lives are dealing with their own brokenness and can, unfortunately, lash out and say hurtful things. Do any of these things you heard as a child still bother you?
Use the page below to write down some of the things you heard as a child.
You'll also need to think about what you would have liked to hear from the adults in your life as a child.

What do you feel your inner child missed out on? Was it hugs, kisses, support, attention, quality time?

How do you think you can give your inner child, the things they missed out on?

What does your inner child need from you in order to feel safe?

What emotion do you run away from the most and why?

Emotions Wheel Exercise

📌 Directions
- Label each section of the wheel with eight different emotions.
- Color in and draw a picture to illustrate what comes to your mind when you see that emotion.
- After completing each section, reflect on why you chose the color and drawing for each emotion.

★ Goal
The purpose of this exercise is to express your emotions without judgement.

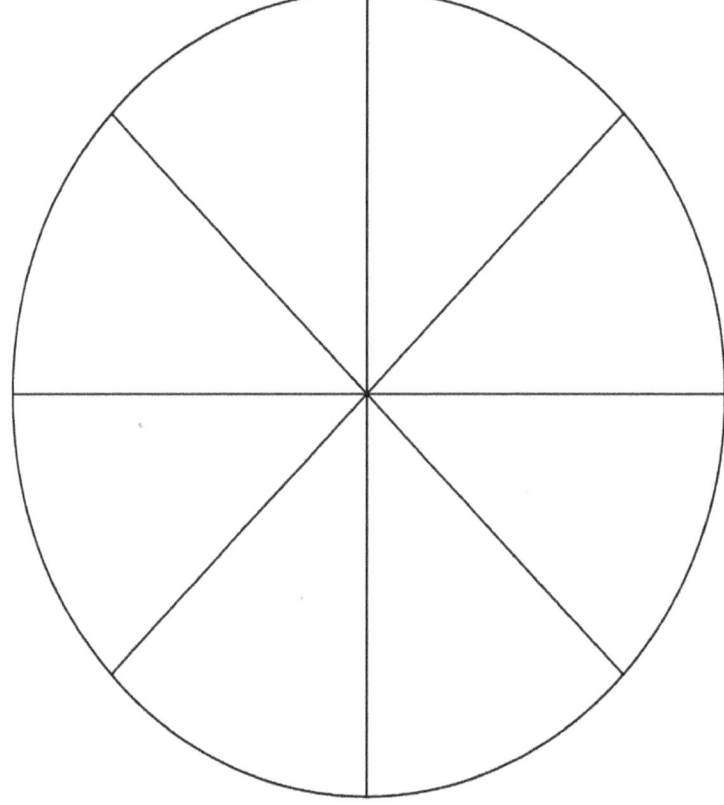

_____

_____

When I Felt Angry As A Child, I Said These Things:

_____	_____
_____	_____
_____	_____
_____	_____
_____	_____
_____	_____

When I Was Angry As A Child, I Did These Things:

_____

_____

_____

_____

_____

_____

_____

When I Feel Angry As An Adult, I Say These Things:

_____	_____
_____	_____
_____	_____
_____	_____
_____	_____

When I Feel Angry As An Adult, I Do These Things:

_____

_____

_____

_____

_____

My Anger Buttons

Fill in each button with something from your childhood that makes you angry. These can be things, situations, or people that "push your buttons."

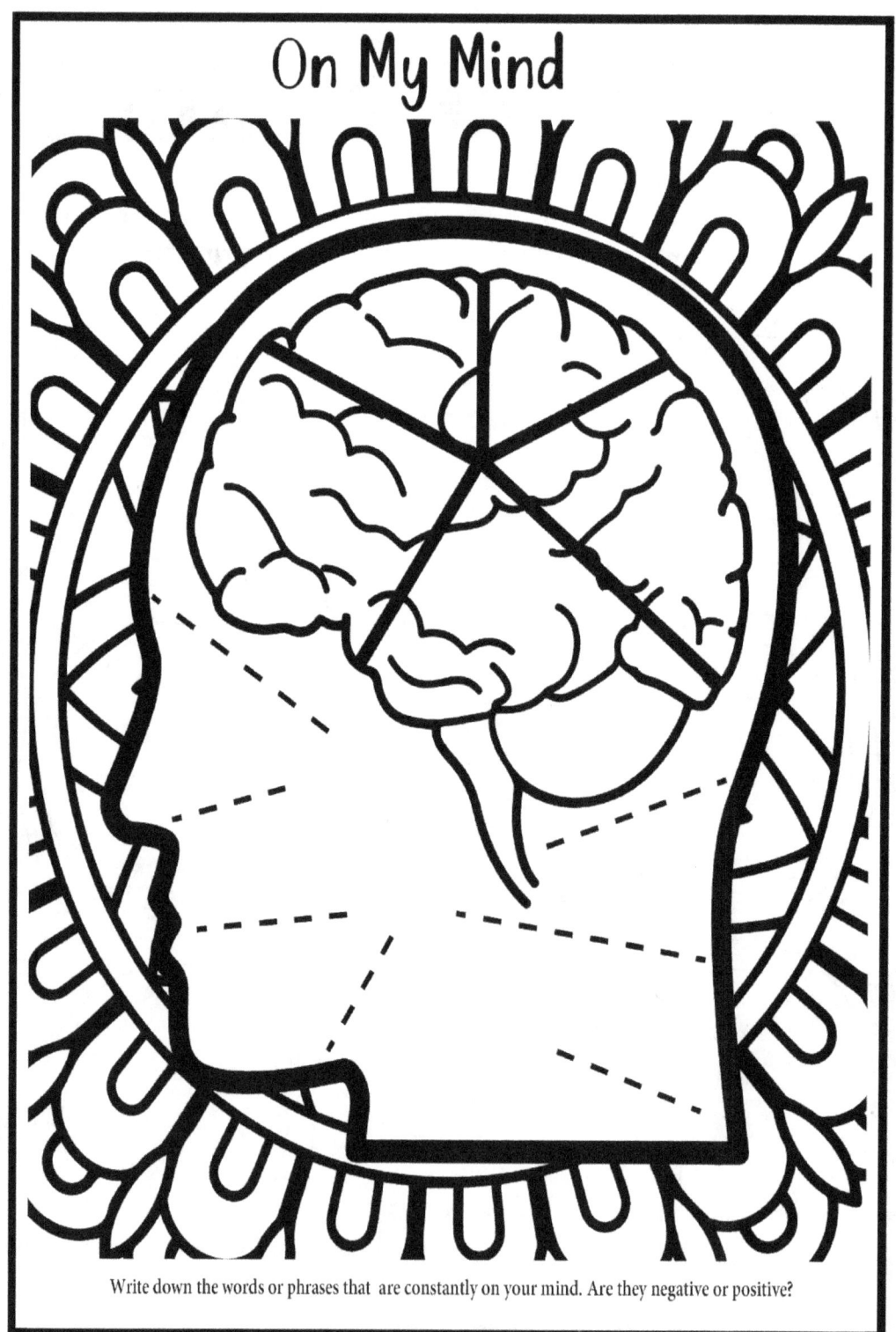

On My Mind

Write down the words or phrases that are constantly on your mind. Are they negative or positive?

How have your childhood traumas harmed your current relationships? Does it negatively impact how you interact with your children? Does it negatively impact your intimate relationships?

_____
_____
_____
_____
_____
_____
_____
_____
_____
_____
_____
_____
_____
_____
_____
_____

Healthy Relationship vs Unhealthy Relationship

Use the space below to fill in what you think a healthy and unhealthy relationship looks like.
Are you currently involved in any unhealthy relationship patterns? What can you do to change this?

Healthy Relationship

☐ _____
☐ _____
☐ _____
☐ _____
☐ _____
☐ _____
☐ _____
☐ _____
☐ _____
☐ _____
☐ _____
☐ _____
☐ _____

Unhealthy Relationship

☐ _____
☐ _____
☐ _____
☐ _____
☐ _____
☐ _____
☐ _____
☐ _____
☐ _____
☐ _____
☐ _____
☐ _____
☐ _____

What are the relationships like that you have with others? (Are you a good friend, loyal employee, etc.)

What are a few examples of how you treat others in relationships?

Do you have a relationship with your inner child? If so, what does it feel like?

What kind of friend can you be to your inner child?

What negative messages have your inner child learned about the world?

How can you ensure your inner child feels validated and safe in relationships?

What is the relationship like that you have with yourself?

Think about what you listed about your relationships with others. Now think about your relationship with yourself. Are you a loyal, supportive, great friend to yourself?

What was your most pleasant experience of self-love?

What was your most painful experience of self-rejection?

When are you the hardest on yourself? How do you punish yourself when you make mistakes?

My "Inner Critic"

We often find that the voice in our head (our inner critic) can be very mean to us at times. You may hear that it calls you names, puts you down, blames you, doubts you, etc. What does your inner critic say to you? Write in the thought bubbles below.

Do you take time to care for yourself, physically and mentally?

What are some promises you've made to yourself that you haven't fulfilled? Does it make *you feel like you've failed yourself ? Why?*

Do you treat others better than you treat yourself? If so, how can this be detrimental?

In what ways can you be more loving towards yourself?

Mirror Me
What do you see when you look in the mirror?

I see someone who is....

Your inner child may need healing and support if you were hurt, neglected, or abused during childhood. Instead of healing, many of us mask the pain our inner child endured. Many people hide their inner child by making it invisible or wearing a mask: use the mask below to depict the mask you wear.

Why do you wear this mask?

Heart Map

Heart mapping! Writing from the heart! Feel in the heart with people, places, and things important to you. Also, be sure to include things that scare you, hold you back, etc. When you're done, color using the color codes from the chart below.

- Red- People, places, or things that bring our negative emotions
- Yellow- People, places, or things I like
- Green- People, places, or things I love

What Does This Love Look Like To You?

Inner Child Storyboard......

1	2
3	4
5	6

Use the storyboard to create a day in the life of your inner child.
What did a typical day in your childhood look like. Use pictures and words in the spaces provided.

What does forgiveness mean to you? Who must you forgive? Why?

What would it take for you to forgive?

Is there something you haven't forgiven yourself for yet?

Is there something you haven't forgiven your parents/caregivers for yet?

What is keeping you from forgiving yourself and others?

What are some things you have a hard time letting go of? They might be grudges, habits, beliefs, etc. Why do you feel like it is difficult to release these things?

_____
_____
_____
_____
_____
_____
_____
_____
_____
_____
_____
_____
_____
_____
_____
_____
_____
_____

LETTING... GO!
Use the balloons to write down things you need to let go of.

What does healing look like to you? Are your expectations for healing helpful for your growth, or do they add more pressure?

The Important Pieces of Your Puzzle

What are the important pieces of your puzzle? What makes you who you are?
Are there any pieces missing that you believe will complete your puzzle?
Use each puzzle piece to write words or draw
the important pieces that make you who you are?

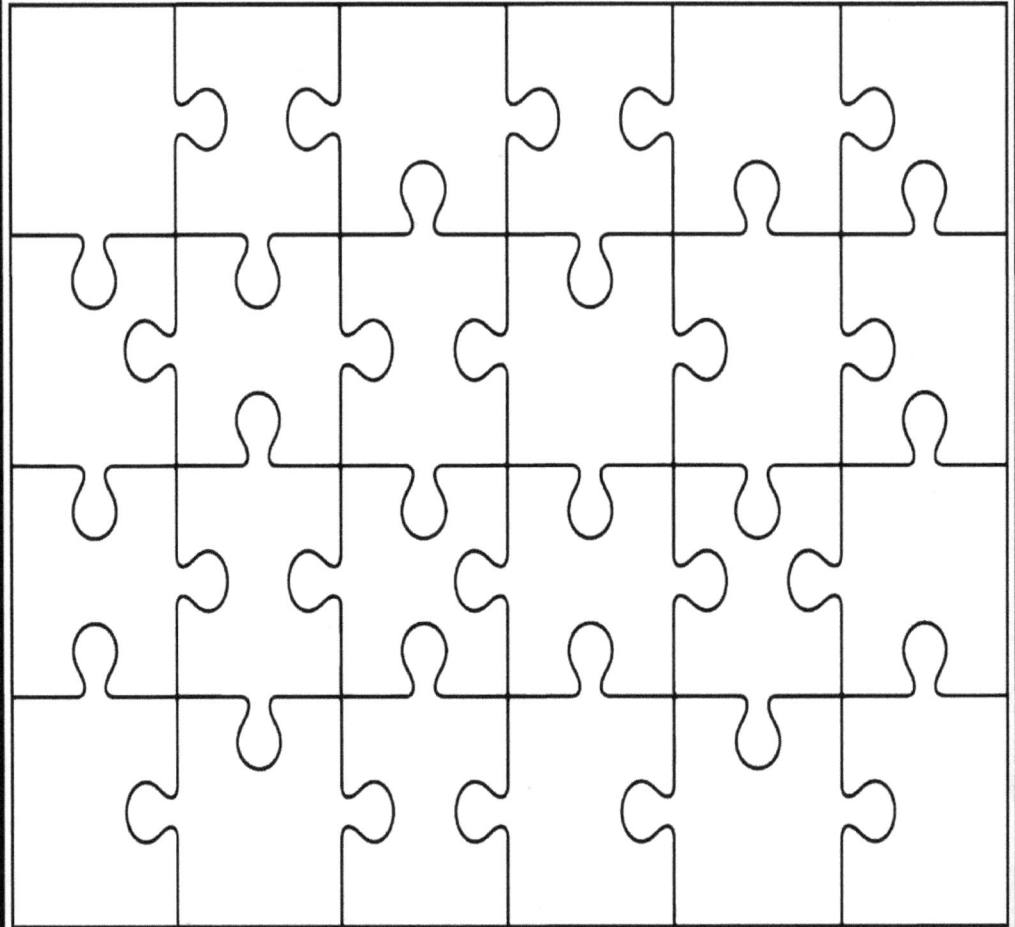

What are the missing pieces of your puzzle?
Why would having these pieces make you feel
complete?

Letter from your inner child....

 Imagine you are writing a letter from your inner child. What would your inner child say to you right now?

Date: _____

Dear: _____

Letter to your adult self

Imagine your inner child is writing a letter to your adult self.
What would you say to your adult self?

Date: _____

Dear: _____

_____

_____

_____

_____

_____

_____

_____

_____

_____

_____

_____

Advice from your adult self
To your inner child

Date: _____

Dear: _____

_____
_____
_____
_____
_____
_____
_____
_____
_____
_____

_____

Apology letter

What I need to hear from the one who hurt me...

Date: _____

Dear: _____

Apology Letter To Myself

Date: _____

Dear: _____

_____
_____
_____
_____
_____
_____
_____
_____
_____
_____
_____
_____

"What I Want To Say"

What Would You Say To This Person If You Knew They Would Listen To Everything You Wanted To Tell Them?

Name:_____

PERSONAL CRISIS PLAN

I Know I'm Triggered When I Notice

_____
_____
_____
_____

Some Good Ways To Distract Myself Are:

Safe People I Can Reach Out To:

1. _____
2. _____
3. _____

Coping Skill I Can Use:

Ways To Keep Myself & My Space Safe:

- _____
- _____
- _____
- _____
- _____
- _____

Other Resources I Can Use To Get Myself Care:

1.
2.
3.

Appreciate These Ten Beautiful Little Things

When your mind is engulfed in worry, it isn't easy to see the truth: Everything is and will be okay. The following are ten little, beautiful things you can appreciate right this second to refocus your mind on the present, easing worry and putting your life into more perspective:

MY ABUSE/TRAUMATIC experiences do not define who I am as a person.

TODAY I choose me.

MY MIND, body, and spirit belong to me.

I RELEASE any th feelings of guilt, hurt, and shame.

LOVE AND TRANQUILITY surround my interactions and my decisions today.

I DO NOT BLAME MYSELF for my childhood experiences/trauma.

I REPLACE HATE, anger, & agitation with others with intentional and positive interactions.

I CHOOSE TO CREATE an atmosphere of peace and safety for myself.

I already survived what I went through.

BOUNDARY setting helps me to create safety within my life.

The Monsters Under My Bed

(List six things that haunted you as a child. Do these things still haunt you today?)

_____
_____
_____
_____
_____
_____

Name some things you fear but still want to do?

How does your inner child feel about the way you have been working towards your goals?

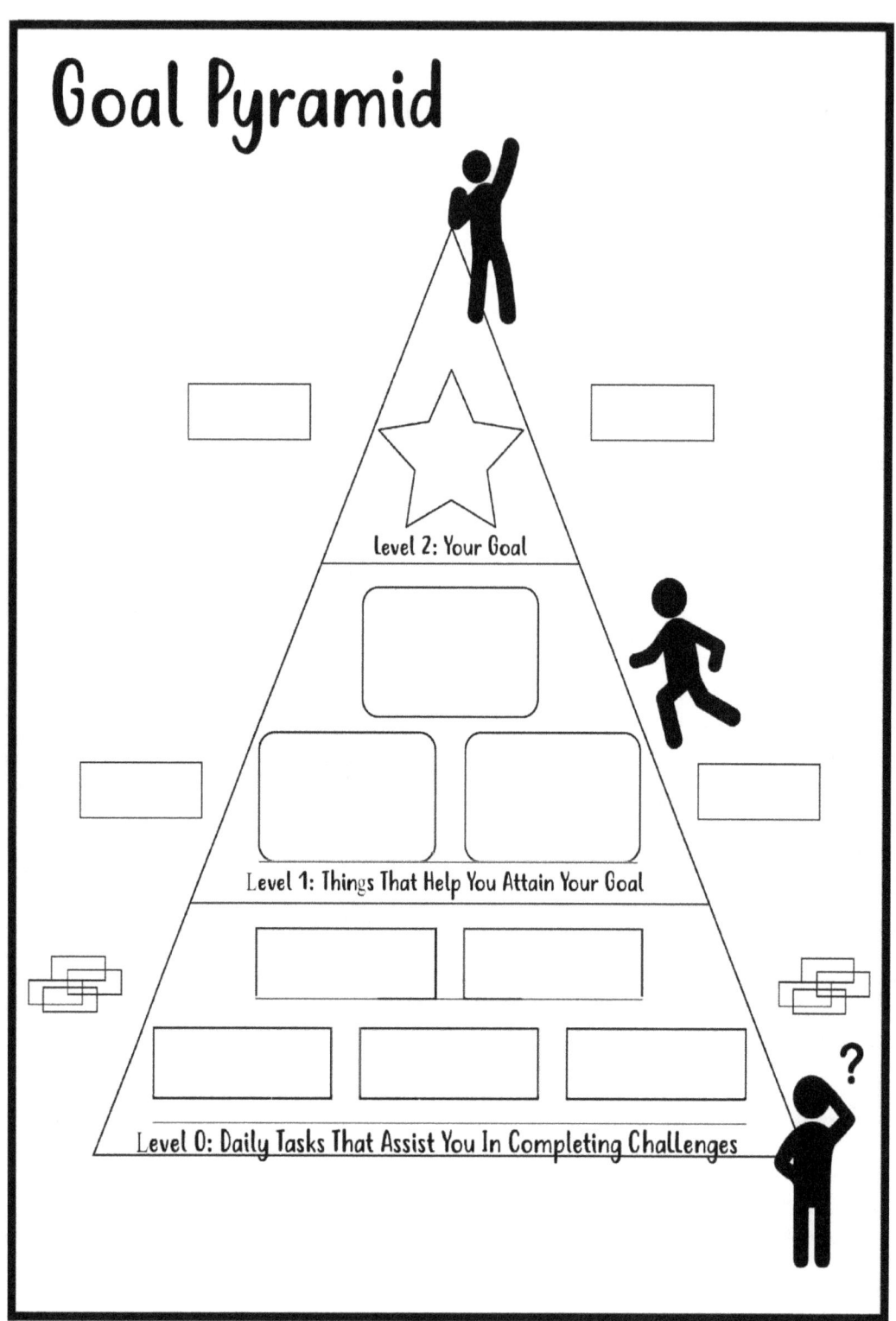

Do your inner child and adult self have any goals in common? If so, what are they?

Child	Adult

How does your inner child think you are doing as an adult?

My adult self bucket list
Check The Things You've Already Done.

- [ ] Swim in each of the four Major Ocean
- [ ] Visit at least three out of The seven new wonders Of the world
- [ ] Go on a week-long cruise
- [ ] Experience the northern lights
- [ ] Hike through the Himalayas
- [ ] Go on a wildlife safari
- [ ] Find a job you love
- [ ] Find a way to love the job you have
- [ ] Negotiate a raise with your boss
- [ ] Tell someone how they've Inspired you
- [ ] Go vegetarian for one month
- [ ] Go vegan for one month
- [ ] Cook all your own meals for two weeks straight
- [ ] Compliment yourself every day in the mirror
- [ ] Go back to school
- [ ] Make a large purchase with only cash
- [ ] Become fluent in a new language
- [ ] Start your own business
- [ ] Take an archery class
- [ ] Get a gym membership

You are not your trauma. What's your legacy?

Name: _____

What will your legacy be? Fill in these stepping stones with things you want people to remember about you. Build your legacy!

Leave a legacy...

Detox —— are there people, places, music, food, objects, or even social apps that stir up negative emotions for you? Create a detox list/plan…

The Road To Abundance

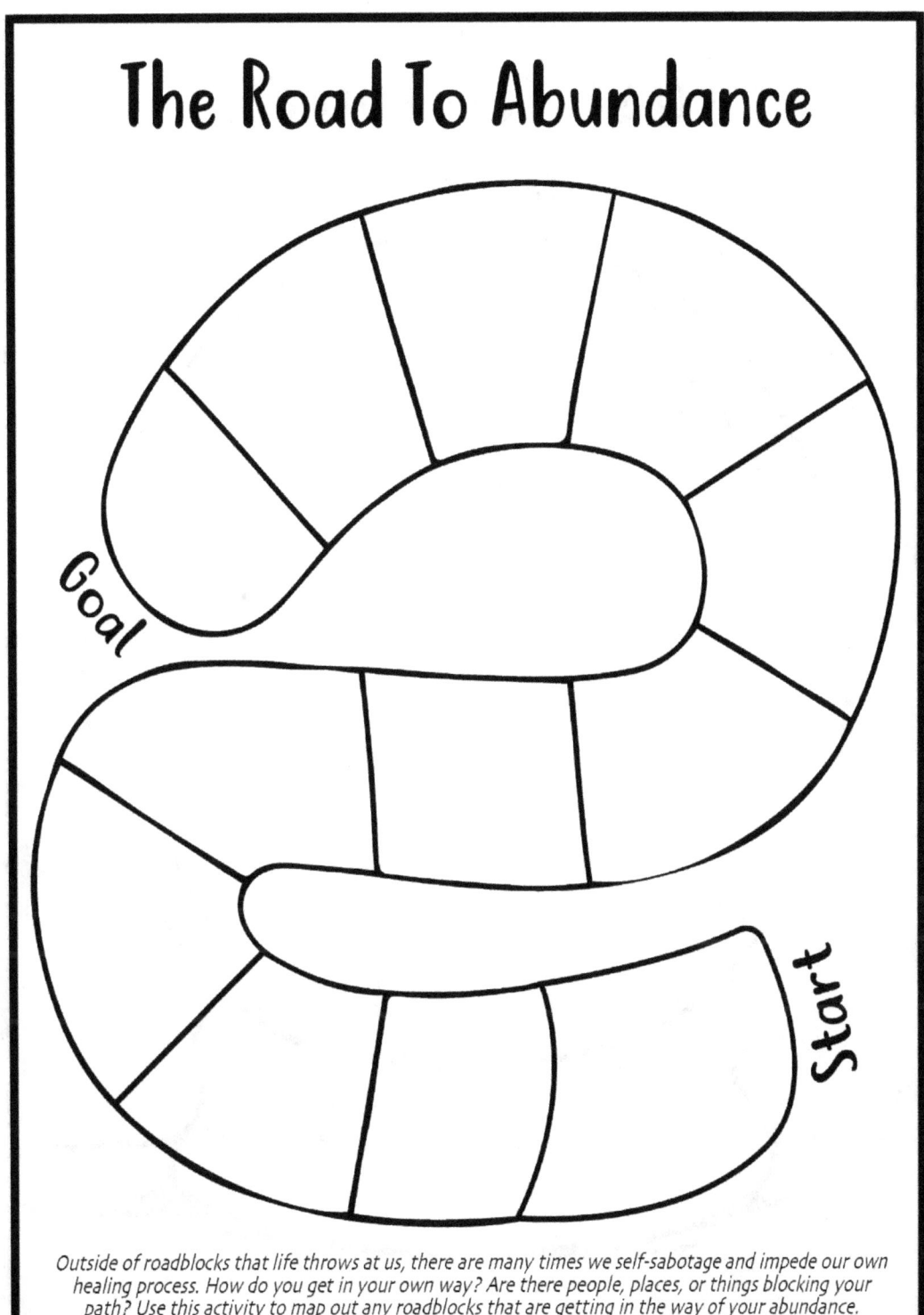

Outside of roadblocks that life throws at us, there are many times we self-sabotage and impede our own healing process. How do you get in your own way? Are there people, places, or things blocking your path? Use this activity to map out any roadblocks that are getting in the way of your abundance.

Fast Forward

Inner child healing work is not all about your past.
Let's think about the future. Where do you see yourself in the next five years?

Reparenting Calendar

Sunday	Monday	Tuesday	Wednesday	Thursday	Friday	Saturday

Daily Reparenting Accountability Chart

	Sunday	Monday	Tuesday	Wednesday	Thursday	Friday	Saturday
1. _____	☐	☐	☐	☐	☐	☐	☐
2. _____	☐	☐	☐	☐	☐	☐	☐
3. _____	☐	☐	☐	☐	☐	☐	☐
4. _____	☐	☐	☐	☐	☐	☐	☐
5. _____	☐	☐	☐	☐	☐	☐	☐
6. _____	☐	☐	☐	☐	☐	☐	☐
7. _____	☐	☐	☐	☐	☐	☐	☐
8. _____	☐	☐	☐	☐	☐	☐	☐

Reparenting Plan

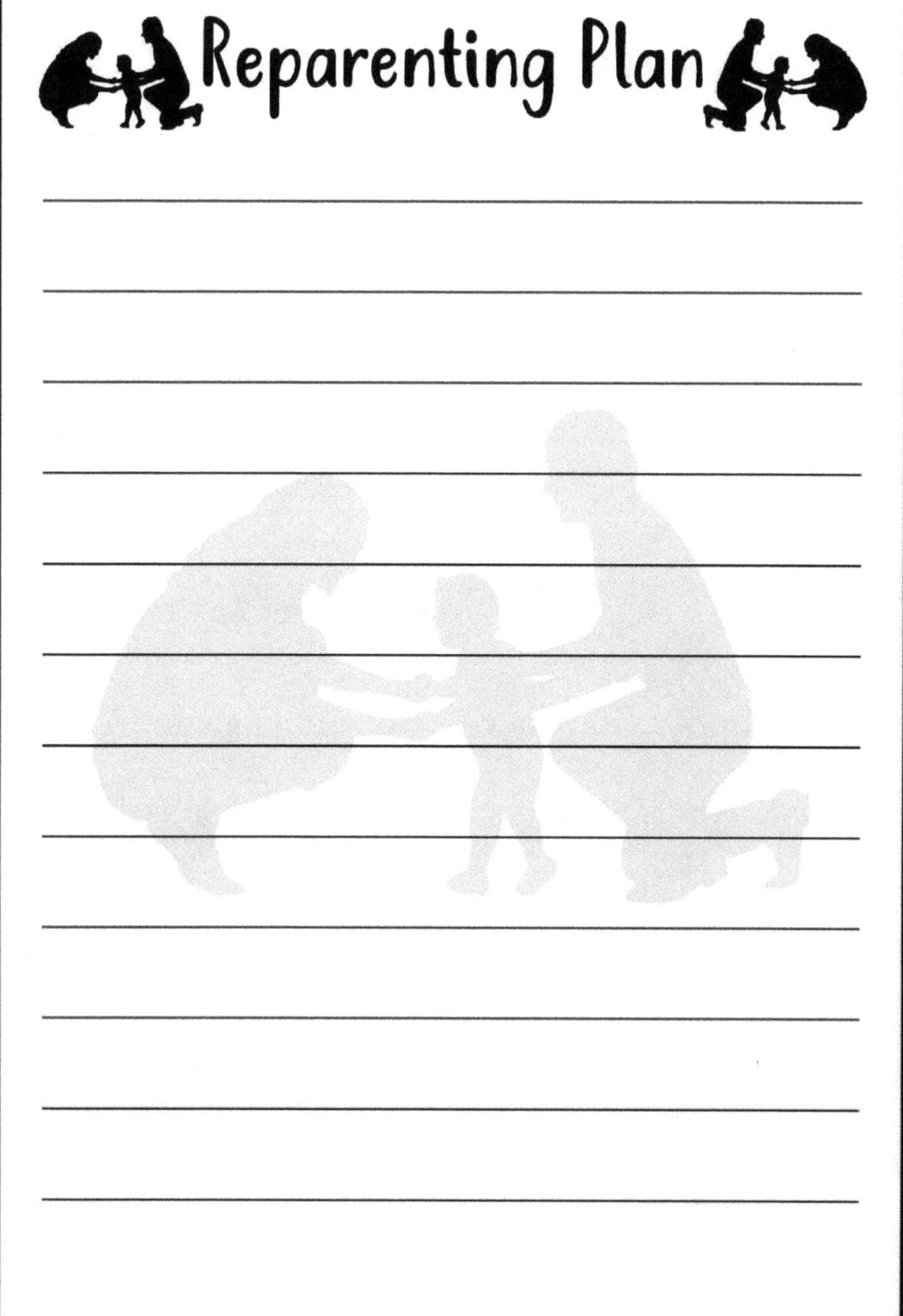

Reparenting Plan

Reparenting Plan

Reparenting Plan

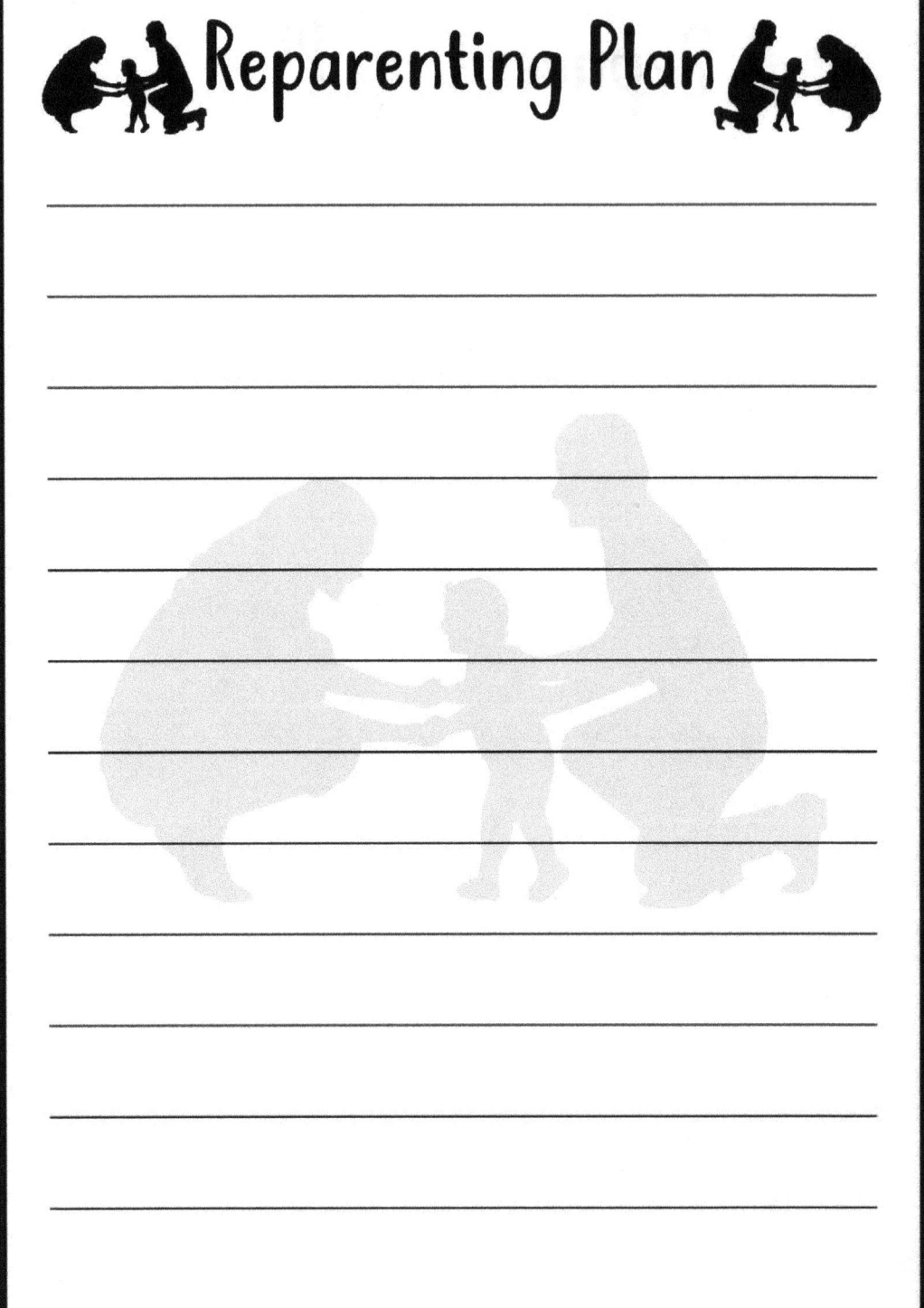

Sunday	Monday	Tuesday	Wednesday	Thursday	Friday	Saturday

Power Playlist

Music has always been a form of therapy.
I'm sure you feel the same way.
What are some songs that make you feel empowered?
List songs that help you heal and remember just how gangsta you are...

IMAGERY
Draw A Happy Ending.

Now that you have an idea of how you would have wanted your story to play out, identify some skills you possess as an adult that can help you resolve childhood conflict for your adult self.

_____
_____
_____
_____
_____
_____
_____
_____
_____
_____
_____
_____
_____
_____
_____
_____
_____
_____

Inner Child Storyboard......

1	2
3	4
5	6

Earlier in the workbook, you created a storyboard of a day in the life of your inner child. Now, I'd like you to rewrite your story using the blank storyboard below

What Is The Theme Song Of Your Life?

Theme: The Main Message, Basis, Story, or Central Idea of Something.

Has Your Theme Song Changed? Why? Why Not?

_____
_____
_____
_____

Acknowledgments

This workbook is a combination of activities and exercises I have either created myself or have used in inner child healing workshops that I have attended by some of the most impactful mental health practitioners around. Thus, I know these simple exercises can help catapult your healing process. Doing inner child work or any type of healing work is not easy. You're forced to deal with some of the hardest moments, eye-opening experiences, and critiques of your life. However, when we can do the work to heal ourselves, something truly magical happens in our lives. I want to acknowledge you for taking steps to transform your life. I'd also like to take the opportunity to thank my children and their father for their support while I was writing this book. To my best friend, who has always been there for me to bounce ideas off of, and the countless editors, illustrators, and graphic designers that I partnered with to bring this book to life, I say thank you. I am forever grateful to every one of you.

References

American Psychological Association. "Mindfulness meditation: A research-proven way to reduce stress." (2019).

Bourbeau, Lise. Heal Your Wounds & Find Your True Self: Rejection, Abandonment, Humiliation, Betrayal, Injustice. Éditions E.T.C. Inc, 2020.

Capacchione, Lucia. Recovery of your inner child: The highly acclaimed method for liberating your inner self. Simon and Schuster, 1991.

Crosson-Tower, Cynthia. Understanding Child Abuse and Neglect Plus MyLab Search with eText -- Access Card Package. Pearson, 2014.

Hanh, Thich Nhat. Reconciliation: Healing the inner child. Parallax Press, 2011.

Jackman, Robert. Healing Your Lost Inner Child: How to Stop Impulsive Reactions, Set Healthy Boundaries and Embrace an Authentic Life. The Art of Practical Wisd, 2020.

McLoyd, Vonnie C. "Socioeconomic disadvantage and child development." American psychologist 53.2 (1998): 185-204.

Moe, Jerry. Understanding addiction and recovery through a child's eyes: Hope, help, and healing for families. Health Communications, Inc., 2007.

Taylor, Cathryn L. The Inner Child Workbook: What to Do with Your Past when it Just Won't Go Away. TarcherPerigee, 1991.

Whitfield, Charles L. Healing the child within: Discovery and recovery for adult children of dysfunctional families. Health Communications, Inc., 2006.

Index

A
accidents, 10
addiction, 6–7
Adult Self, 2, 21–22, 40–41, 115, 147
Anger buttons, 75
angry, 6, 15, 73–75
Apology letter, 117, 119

B
betrayed trust, 11
bullying, 10, 13

C
challenging feelings, 26
Child self, 40–41
childhood
    memories, 63
    Timeline, 34
    trauma, 8, 10–12, 17–18, 37, 64, 77, 101
    triggers, 15–19
cognitive behavioral therapists, 25
compassion, 1, 17, 25–29
confidence, 1, 13–14
courage, 13

D
detox list/plan, 134
divorce, 13
domestic violence, 10
Dyer, Wayne, 32

E
emotional
    abuse, 4, 8
    memories, 48
    triggers, 17
Emotions Wheel exercise, 72
empathy, 1, 28

F
failure, 1, 8, 13, 22
family tree, 42
father, 56–62
flashbacks, 17
forgiveness, 28–29, 102
frustrating event, 10

G
Goal pyramid, 128

H
healthy relationship, 8, 21, 26, 78
Heart map, 98
humiliating situation, 10

I
Imagery, 146
imagination, 24
injuries, 10, 12
Inner Child Drawing, 38
inner critic, 29, 90
Intention setting worksheet, 32
Internal family systems therapy, 4

J
Jungian shadow work, 4

K
kindness, 28–29

L
legacy, 133
life-threatening illness, 10

M
meditating, 27
monsters, 125
mother, 49–55

N
natural disaster/war, 13
negative messages, 83

P
pain, 1, 7–8, 96
panic attacks, 17
personal crisis plan, 122
physical abuse, 12
pleasure in learning, 24
post-traumatic stress disorder (PTSD), 13
poverty, 11
power playlist, 144
Psychoanalytic Psychotherapy, 4

R
re-parenting, 2, 26–27, 31
re-traumatizing situations, 16
reality check, 37
relationship counselor, 27
relationship with your mother, 49–50, 53
relationships, 2, 4, 11, 21, 77–80, 84

Reparenting
    Accountability Chart, 138
    calendar, 137
    plan, 139
romantic breakup, 10

S
self-care plan, 16
self-compassion, 17, 25, 29
self-confidence, 1
self-esteem, 13–14
self-medication, 6
self-rejection, 88
serious accident, 14
sexual abuse, 11–12
Somatic Experiencing Therapy, 4
surgery, 10

T
theme song, 36, 151
trauma, 4–18, 101, 133
trauma triggers, 15–16
traumatic accident, 8

U
unhealthy relationship, 78

V
violent, 10
voice of truth, 101

www.ingramcontent.com/pod-product-compliance
Lightning Source LLC
Chambersburg PA
CBHW081205170426
43197CB00018B/2924